Football Player

Facts for Fun!

Wide Receivers

By Wyatt Michaels

Copyright 2013

All rights reserved.

No duplication without the express written permission of the author.

Image courtesy of bterrycompton

Who had the most receptions in his rookie season?

- A. Anquan Boldin
- B. Victor Cruz
- C. Wes Welker

Image courtesy of Social Responsibility

The answer is A. Anquan Boldin

Anquan had 101 receptions in his rookie season of 2003.

Image courtesy of woodleywonderworks

Who was the first to have 20 or more touchdown receptions in one year?

   A. Jerry Rice
   B. Randy Moss
   C. Sterling Sharpe

Image courtesy of fabfiver5

The answer is A. Jerry Rice

Jerry had 22 touchdown receptions in 1987. His record was broken by Randy Moss in 2007 with 23.

Image courtesy of wickenden

Who had the most receptions in one game?

A. Calvin Johnson
B. Torry Holt
C. Brandon Marshall

Image courtesy of gtalan

The answer is C. Brandon Marshall

Brandon had 21 receptions in one game in 2009.

Image courtesy of Caitlinator

Who holds the record for the most touchdowns in one month?

- A. Danny Amendola
- B. Jerry Rice
- C. Reggie Wayne

Image courtesy of Social Responsibility

The answer is B. Jerry Rice

Jerry had 10 touchdown receptions in one month in 1987.

Image courtesy of SD Dirk

Who has the most consecutive games with 10 or more pass receptions?

A. Anquan Boldin
B. Andre Johnson
C. Brandon Marshall

Image courtesy of M Glasgow

The answer is B. Andre Johnson

Andre Johnson had 3 consecutive games with 10+ receptions in 2008.

Image courtesy of Vironevaeh

Who has the most consecutive games with 3 or more pass receptions?

    A. Calvin Johnson
    B. Cris Carter
    C. Reggie Wayne

Image courtesy of Jeffrey Beall

The answer is C. Reggie Wayne

Reggie is still adding to his record of 64 consecutive games at the end of the 2012 season.

Image courtesy of spakattacks

Who has the most touchdowns in his rookie season?

A. Jerry Rice
B. Randy Moss
C. Terrell Owens

Image courtesy of jdn

The answer is B. Randy Moss

Randy had 17 touchdowns in his rookie season of 1998.

Image courtesy of bazhall81

Who has had the most seasons with 110 or more receptions?

A. Randy Moss
B. Terrell Owens
C. Wes Welker

Image courtesy of sportiqe

The answer is C. Wes Welker

Wes has had 5 consecutive seasons of at least 110 receptions from 2007-2012 as of the end of the regular season 2012. In 2009 and 2011 he had over 120 receptions.

Image courtesy of Psykotrooper

Who had the most consecutive seasons with 15 or more touchdown receptions?

A. Marvin Harrison
B. Michael Irvin
C. Jerry Rice

Image courtesy of Glenn's GISuser

The answer is C. Jerry Rice

This is one of many records that Jerry Rice holds. He scored over 15 receiving touchdowns in 1986 and 1987.

Image courtesy of public domain

Who has the most seasons with at least 17 touchdown receptions?

A. Randy Moss
B. Michael Irvin
C. Sterling Sharpe

Image courtesy of Keith Allison

The answer is A. Randy Moss

Randy has had at least 17 touchdown receptions in 3 different seasons (1998, 2003, and 2007). No one has had more years, or more touchdown receptions - ever.

Image courtesy of mlabowicz

Who holds the record for the most touchdowns in one season?

   A. Anquan Boldin
   B. Randy Moss
   C. Victor Cruz

Image courtesy of rezsox

The answer is B. Randy Moss

Randy had 23 touchdowns in 2007.

Image courtesy of Ed Yourdon

Who had the highest average gain in one game (with at least three receptions)?

- A. Tony Gonzalez
- B. Torry Holt
- C. Anquan Boldin

Image courtesy of GMO66

The answer is B. Torry Holt

Torry had a game September 24, 2000 with at least three receptions, and averaged 63 yards per reception.

Image courtesy of Neon Tommy

Who shares the record for the most consecutive games with 2 or more touchdown receptions?

A. Calvin Johnson
B. Dwayne Bowe
C. Torry Holt

Image courtesy of Mike Morbeck

The answer is A. Calvin Johnson

Calvin and Cris Carter share the record of 4 consecutive games with at least 2 touchdown receptions.

Image courtesy of dionhinchcliffe

Who holds the record for the most receptions in a single season?

A. Calvin Johnson
B. Marvin Harrison
C. Reggie Wayne

Image courtesy of Matt McGee

The answer is B. Marvin Harrison

Marvin had 143 receptions in 2002.

Image courtesy of nerissa's ring

Who holds the record for the most consecutive seasons with at least 4 touchdown receptions?

A. Randy Moss
B. Terrell Owens
C. Tony Gonzalez

Image courtesy of public domain

The answer is B. Terrell Owens

Terrell had 15 consecutive seasons with at least 4 touchdown receptions from 1996 to 2010.

Image courtesy of bazhall81

Who has the most games with 18 receptions?

    A. Brandon Marshall
    B. Dwayne Bowe
    C. Marvin Harrison

Image courtesy of public domain

The answer is A. Brandon Marshall

Brandon has had two games with 18 receptions -- from 2008 to 2012.

Image courtesy of West Point Public Affairs

Who is one of seven players to win the "Triple Crown" at the receiver position? (The Triple Crown is leading the league in receiving yards, receiving touchdowns, and receptions.)

A. Randy Moss
B. Sterling Sharpe
C. Torry Holt

Image courtesy of mwibbels

The answer is B. Sterling Sharpe

The other six players to win the Triple Crown are Don Hutson, Elroy Hirsch, Pete Pihos, Raymond Berry, Jerry Rice and Steve Smith.

Image courtesy of moodboardphotography

Thirteen receivers have a 99 yard touchdown, but who has a 99 yard touchdown with the most yards after the catch?

A. Reggie Wayne
B. Victor Cruz
C. Wes Welker

Image courtesy of JrzyKat

The answer is B. Victor Cruz

Victor ran 89 yards after the catch to score a touchdown in December 2011 against the New York Jets.

Image courtesy of Schlusselbein2007

Who holds the record for being the fastest to record 600 career receptions?

A. Anquan Boldin
B. Cris Carter
C. Sterling Sharpe

Image courtesy of Iswiecicki

The answer is A. Anquan Boldin

It only took Anquan 98 games to reach 600 receptions.

Image courtesy of Erik Daniel Drost

Who has the most games with 13 receptions?

A. Anquan Boldin
B. Victor Cruz
C. Wes Welker

Image courtesy of jdn

The answer is C. Wes Welker

Wes has had 5 games with at least 13 receptions from 2004-2012.

Image courtesy of RLEVANS

Who holds the record for the most consecutive seasons with at least 10 touchdown receptions?

A. Brandon Marshall
B. Marvin Harrison
C. Jerry Rice

Image courtesy of Djmunden

The answer is B. Marvin Harrison

Marvin had 8 consecutive seasons with at least 10 touchdown receptions from 1999-2006.

Image courtesy of Navin75

Who holds the record for Super Bowl rookie receptions and receiving yards?

A. Jerry Rice
B. Reggie Wayne
C. Torry Holt

Image courtesy of public domain

The answer is C. Torry Holt

Torry had 7 receptions and 109 receiving yards in the Super Bowl of his rookie season in 1999.

Congratulations! You are now an expert on NFL wide receivers. Impress or quiz your fellow football fans with this book or Football Player Facts for Fun! Quarterbacks.

Look for more quiz books by Wyatt Michaels about baseball, letter sounds, careers, dogs, horses, presidents, states, and more.

Made in the USA
Coppell, TX
20 March 2023